TIME
FOR KIDS

Writer's Notebook

By the Editors of TIME For Kids

Teacher Created Materials
PUBLISHING

TCM 10148 (i1035)

**TIME For Kids® Writer's Notebook
Level C**
Copyright © 2006
Time Inc.

TIME For Kids and the Red Border Design are registered trademarks of Time Inc. All rights reserved. Developed in collaboration with *Exploring Writing* and distributed by Teacher Created Materials Publishing.

TIME For Kids
Editorial Director: Keith Garton
Editor: Jonathan Rosenbloom
Project Editor: The Quarasan Group, Inc.
Design Production: The Quarasan Group, Inc.
Illustrator: The Quarasan Group, Inc.
Teacher Reviewers: Brian Glassman, MD; Nancy Kern, VA; Vincent LaRuina, NY; Greg Matchett, AZ; Jana Miller, TX; JoAnne Winnick, CA

Exploring Writing™
Copyright © 2006
Teacher Created Materials Publishing

Teacher Created Materials Publishing
Publisher: Rachelle Cracchiolo, M.S. Ed.
Editor-in-Chief: Sharon Coan, M.S. Ed.
Editorial Project Manager: Dona Herweck Rice

ISBN: 978-0-7439-0148-2

Teacher Created
Materials Publishing
5301 Oceanus Drive
Huntington Beach, CA 92649
www.tcmpub.com

Photography credits:
Page 1: PhotoDisc, Inc.; p.5: PhotoDisc, Inc.; p.6: Comstock; p.8: Corel; p.9: Corel; p.10: (b) Corel, (r) PhotoDisc, Inc.; p.11: (b) Corel, (tr) Artville, (bl) PhotoDisc, Inc.; p.12: Corel; p.14: (l) Corbis, (c) Corbis, (r) Corbis; p.16: (t) Corel, (c) Corbis; p.18: PhotoDisc, Inc.; p.19: Corbis; p.20: (b) PhotoDisc, Inc., (t) ComStock; p.21: MetaCreations/Kai Power Photos; p.24: (t) Jeremy, (b) Nicole, (bkgd) ComStock; p.25: MetaCreations/Kai Power Photos; p.28: PhotoDisc, Inc.; p.34: Corbis; 35: Corbis; p.36: Corbis; p.38: (t) Diamar Portfolios, (c) Corbis; p.38- 39 (bkgd) Corel; p.39: PhotoDisc, Inc.; p.40 (b) PhotoDisc, Inc., (t) Artville, LLC; p.41: PhotoDisc, Inc.; p.42: Artville, LLC; p.44: PhotoDisc, Inc.; p.45: PhotoDisc, Inc. p.45: PhotoDisc, Inc.; p.46: PhotoDisc, Inc.; p.47: (t) PhotoDisc, Inc., (b) PhotoDisc, Inc.; p.48: ComStock; p.49: (b) Corel, (c) MetaCreations/Kai Power Photos; p.51: MetaCreations/Kai Power Photos; p.55: ComStock; p.57: PhotoDisc, Inc. p.61: PhotoDisc, Inc. p.63: PhotoDisc, Inc. p.67: PhotoDisc, Inc.; p.70 (l) PhotoDisc, Inc., (r) PhotoDisc, Inc.; p.72: PhotoDisc, Inc.; p.73: Corbis; p.76: Corel; p.77: Artville; p.78: MetaCreations/Kai Power Photos; p.80 PhotoDisc, Inc.; p.81: (bkgd) ComStock, (tl) PhotoDisc, Inc., (tr) PhotoDisc, Inc., (bl) PhotoDisc, Inc., (br) PhotoDisc, Inc.; p.82: PhotoDisc, Inc.; p.83: (bknd) Comstock, (r) PhotoDisc, Inc.; p.84: Comstock; p.95 PhotoDisc, Inc.; p.96: PhotoDisc, Inc.

 For more writing practice: www.timeforkids.com/hh/writeideas

Table of Contents

Using Your Writer's Notebook **5**

Steps in the Writing Process **6**

Prewriting • Drafting • Revising • Editing and Proofreading • Publishing

Section 1: Prewriting **13**

Getting Started • Be a List Keeper • Choose a Topic • Think About It • Organize Your Ideas

Section 2: Drafting **23**

What Is a First Draft? • A Sample First Draft

Time to Write Fiction 26
What Is Fiction? • Story Elements

Time to Write Nonfiction 32
What Is Nonfiction? • Finding Information • Including Main Ideas and Supporting Details • Fact or Opinion? • Essay • Interview • Writing to Persuade • Strong Openings and Closings

Time to Write Poetry 50

Section 3: Revising 53

Time to Revise • Time to Write a Title • Time to Write a
Beginning • Time to Make the Meaning Clear • Time to Put
Words in Order • Time to Choose Strong Nouns • Time to Use
Vivid Verbs • Time to Add Adjectives • Time to Add Adverbs

Section 4: Editing and Proofreading 65

Writing Great Sentences • A Sentence for Every Reason •
Writing a Paragraph • Focus on Capital Letters • Focus on
Punctuation • Check Your Spelling • Using Proofreading Marks

Section 5: Publishing 79

What to Publish • Publishing on a Computer • Planning a
Multimedia Presentation

Vocabulary 85

Index 92

Traits of Good Writing Index 96

Using Your Writer's Notebook

Do you know how to face the blank page with confidence? Becoming a better writer is like becoming a better athlete. You practice, practice, and then practice some more. The secret to good writing is to keep writing—anywhere, everywhere, and all the time.

At TIME For Kids, writers go through many of the same challenges that you do as you write. TFK writers must find topics that will interest readers, research the facts, organize their ideas, and write a draft. Then they revise, edit, and proofread their writing. Think of writing as a process, steps that help you become a better writer. Look for tips from the TFK writers throughout this book.

Your TIME For Kids Writer's Notebook is a handy tool you can use when you write. In your Notebook, you will find

- a guide to the writing process, featuring a section about each of the steps that good writers follow.

- mini-lessons on skills such as main idea and supporting details.

- samples of different kinds of writing, from how-to articles to fiction.

- lists of words that will make your writing clear and interesting.

Remember, have fun with your writing. Find a topic that matters to you and makes you want to write. Use your TFK Writer's Notebook for tips and examples to help you become a better writer. Jot down your ideas. Try out new ways of expressing yourself. Make this Notebook your very own guide for good writing.

Time to Write: The Writing Process

Steps in the Writing Process

1 Prewriting—Think and plan. Choose a topic and brainstorm ideas. Organize your ideas. Consider your audience and think about the best way to communicate your message.

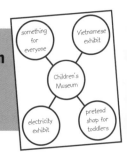

2 Drafting—Get your ideas down on paper. Use the plan you developed in Prewriting to create sentences and paragraphs. Write with enthusiasm and confidence.

Revising—Share and reflect on your first draft. Use responses from other readers to improve your writing. Add vivid words that say exactly what you mean.

Editing and Proofreading—Find and correct any mistakes you have made. Check your spelling, capitalization, and punctuation. Be sure you have used words correctly.

Publishing—Choose a way to present your best writing for others to enjoy.

TFK Tips for Writers

Are you having trouble finding ideas to write about? Look around your school and neighborhood. Talk to friends. Read a news magazine. Try the Internet.

Now let's take a closer look at each step in the writing process.

Prewriting

Prewriting is the time to think, plan, and organize your ideas about a topic you have chosen. You may want to use a graphic organizer to arrange your ideas and plan how the details fit together. For example, you can use a web to show how ideas are related.

Remember, there are many different ways of organizing your writing. When you write a story, it is usually important to tell events in the order in which they happen. If you are comparing two similar things, you might tell all the ways they are alike in one paragraph, and then write another paragraph that explains the differences. A persuasive essay might begin with an opinion, followed by reasons that support that point of view listed in order of importance. Every time you write, choose a type of organization that fits the topic and your purpose for writing.

something for everyone

Vietnamese exhibit

Children's Museum

electricity exhibit

pretend shop for toddlers

Tip for Using Writer's Voice

TFK Managing Editor **Martha Pickerill** says, "As a reporter, once I've gathered and organized the information, I ask myself, 'How would I tell this story out loud to someone I know?'"

Drafting

Drafting is the time to write. Use your organizer or notes from the prewriting step to write sentences and paragraphs. Think about what you will say to accomplish your purpose. Keep your audience in mind. When you write your first draft, don't worry too much about spelling, capital letters, or punctuation. Your writing doesn't have to be perfect. You can correct mistakes later.

A Museum

There's a teenager watching a Vietnamese fairy tale. Next to him, there is a toddler and a mother looking at an exibat about electricity they call it the Children's Museum of Houston, but really it is for everyone.

TFK Tip from a Pro

James Poniewozik, Staff Writer for *TIME* magazine, says, "It's important to force yourself to write, however bad the writing might be, and know that you can go back and improve it. If you're not writing anything, you'll never finish! Sometimes you just have to force the words out, kind of like warming yourself up when you are exercising. Then, once you're warmed up, you can move ahead and refine it, make it what you want it to be."

Revising

Revising is the time to make your writing better. With a partner, reflect on what you have written. Does the opening entice your readers to continue reading? Do exact words and interesting details help them picture what is happening? Are the ideas presented in a way that makes sense? Listen to your partner's comments. Use the responses to improve your draft. What changes did the writer make to improve the draft on page 9?

A Museum Just for Kids

In one corner you see a teenager mesmerized by a Vietnamese fairy tale. Next to him, there is a toddler pretending to shop and a mother entranced by an exibat about electricity they call it the Children's Museum of Houston, but really it is for everyone.

TFK Tip from a Pro

TFK Assistant Managing Editor **Nellie Gonzalez Cutler** says, "Revising is one of the most important parts of the writing process. After I've written a first draft of a story, I reread it carefully. Then I mark the areas that need work. After making corrections on my first draft, I write a second draft and repeat the entire process. . . Remember: write, read, revise, and repeat!"

Editing and Proofreading

Editing and Proofreading is the time to find and correct any mistakes before you make a final copy of your writing. Be sure that you have written complete sentences and used correct punctuation. Look for errors in using capital letters. Find and correct any words that were misspelled. Notice how the writer used proofreading marks to show what needed to be fixed.

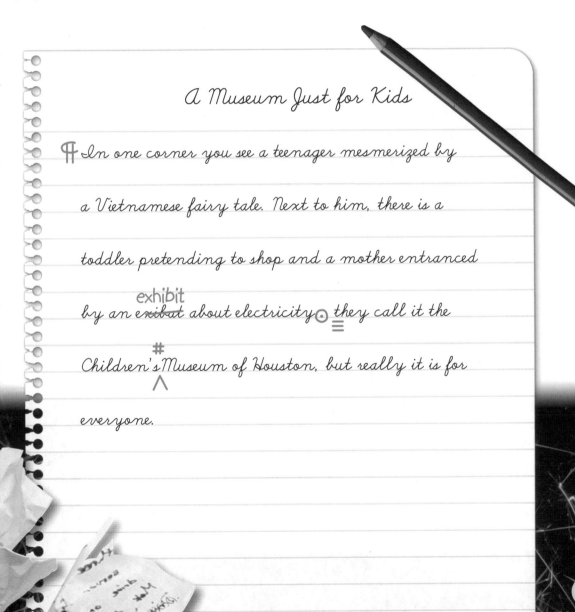

A Museum Just for Kids

¶In one corner you see a teenager mesmerized by a Vietnamese fairy tale. Next to him, there is a toddler pretending to shop and a mother entranced by an exhibit about electricity⊙ they call it the Children's Museum of Houston, but really it is for everyone.

Publishing

Publishing is the time to write your final copy and present it to others. There are many ways to share your writing. For example, you might make a booklet to tell your story or submit an article to your school newspaper. When deciding how to publish something you have written, think about your purpose for writing and the audience you want to reach. Remember that writers publish only their best work.

A Museum Just for Kids

In one corner you see a teenager mesmerized by a Vietnamese fairy tale. Next to him, there is a toddler pretending to shop and a mother entranced by an exhibit about electricity. They call it the Children's Museum of Houston, but really it is for everyone.

1

Prewriting

Time to plan and organize what you are going to write about

Getting Started

Do you have trouble coming up with ideas to write about? Good writers get their ideas from the world around them.

Tune In

Close your eyes and then quickly open them. How would you describe the place you are right now? Do you see a brightly colored display or tree branches swaying in the breeze? Do you hear voices chattering or a plane passing overhead? Is the aroma of pizza making you hungry?

Use your senses to tune into the world around you. You will discover many interesting subjects to write about in your neighborhood, school, town, or city. Write about what is most familiar to you—people you know, places you have been, and issues that have special meaning for you.

Be a Word Collector

Many writers keep lists of favorite words. These might include words that create a mood, express a feeling, describe an action, or simply have a fun sound. Where can you find these words? Read books. Listen to the news. Have conversations. Then make notes about the great words you see and hear.

Try This!

Start your own personal writer's notebook. Keep it close at hand so you can record interesting experiences and write new words that you encounter. Warm up by adding to the list of favorite words. Learn the meaning of the words you list, and try to use them in your writing.

My Favorite Words

1 scrumptious

2 jumbo

3 consternation

4 _____

5 _____

6 _____

Anywhere, Anytime

You can write anywhere, anytime. Use a notebook, sticky notes, even your Writer's Notebook. Jot down lines from favorite books, or phrases that describe unusual sights. Look at the ideas recorded by one writer. What might you add?

Favorite Lines from Movies

"My dear Professor, I've never seen a cat sit so stiffly." [**Dumbledore,** in *Harry Potter and the Sorcerer's Stone*]

"As you wish." [**Westley** in *The Princess Bride*]

_____

_____

_____

_____

_____

Unusual Sights

Egrets, pelicans, ducks—all at once hundreds of birds skidded to a halt on the surface of the pond!

_____

_____

_____

Refer to your notes when you need to come up with a topic. Recall experiences you have had. Think about favorite stories. Keep a journal to collect ideas to write about. Ask others what they would like to read about.

Tip from a Time For Kids reporter

Jill Marie Egan says, "My favorite place to write is my journal because I can say anything I want and nobody knows or cares."

Be a List Keeper

Good writers are often list keepers. The words they collect suggest ideas for topics to write about. How would you add to the lists on this page?

Places I'd Like to See

1 the new zoo in town

2 the Leaning Tower of Pisa

3 _____

4 _____

5 _____

Big Cats

1 lions

2 cheetahs

3 _____

4 _____

5 _____

My Pet Peeves

1 nosy people

2 litter in the park

3 _____

4 _____

5 _____

Try This!

Here are some more lists to complete.

People I Admire

1 Martin Luther King, Jr.

2 Oprah Winfrey

3 _____

4 _____

5 _____

Issues I Feel Strongly About

1 volunteering in my community

2 eating healthy foods

3 _____

4 _____

5 _____

My Favorite Activities

1 riding a horse

2 making blueberry pancakes

3 _____

4 _____

5 _____

Time to Write

Make your own list. Give your list a title. Use this and your other lists when you
need to find a topic to write about.

Title: _____

1 _____ **4** _____

2 _____ **5** _____

3 _____ **6** _____

Choose a Topic

You're facing a blank page. How do you get started? Begin by looking back at your lists. Choose an idea that would make a good topic. Be sure it's a topic you are excited about—a cause you believe in, a person you admire, or a place you really want to visit.

Think of a Title

What do you want to say about your topic? Create a title that hints at your topic and grabs your readers' attention. A title will help you focus on the main idea you want to communicate. You can always choose a new title later if your topic changes.

Look at these sample titles. Discuss with a partner what you think the topic might be.

No Place to Roam   *Who's Who in the New Zoo*
Eat Your Way to Good Health   *Why I Admire Martin Luther King, Jr.*

Try This!

One writer started a list of possible topics for a story. What topics would you add? Refer to your word lists for ideas.

- a flying squirrel   • _____
- fun on a rainy day   • _____
- a unique animal   • _____

Write a title for a story about your own topic or one of the topics above.

_____

TFK Tips for Writers

When you're searching for a topic to write about, brainstorm ideas with a partner. Let your imagination run wild!

Narrow It Down

Some topics are too big to write about because there is too much to say. Before you begin, you may need to narrow your topic, or break it into smaller parts. Try an organizer like the one shown here. Put the broad topic at the top. Keep narrowing it until you have a topic you can write about easily in one piece of writing.

Animals → too big!

Mammals of Asia → better

Bengal Tiger → just right

Next, decide if you know enough to write about your topic. Do you need references to find more information? Below are some helpful resources.

- An **encyclopedia** provides information on many topics, arranged in alphabetical order.

- An **atlas** is a book of maps.

- Internet **Web sites** can give up-to-date information on a wide variety of topics from many sources.

- **Nonfiction books** provide facts about real people or events.

Try This!

What references would you choose to learn more about Bengal tigers? Use one to find reliable information on the topic. Share with a classmate one or two facts that you find in your search.

TFK Tips for Writers

Read about your topic. If it seems too big, focus on a small part of the topic that is especially interesting to you.

Think About It

After you choose and narrow a topic, think about what you want to say and how to say it. Ask yourself questions as you prepare to write.

Why am I writing? Do I want to persuade people to take action on a certain issue? describe an exciting experience? inform about a current event? entertain with a rhyme?

What am I writing? Am I writing an adventure story? an interview for the school newspaper? a narrative about a frightening experience?

Who is my audience? Am I writing for my teacher? a close friend? my grandmother?

Why?
entertain, inform, persuade
describe

What?
an interview, a poem, an essay,
a personal narrative

My audience?
teacher, friend, the class

Try This!

Before you begin writing, make a plan. Use the questions on this page to determine your purpose and decide what to write.

Organize Your Ideas

You've chosen a topic and listed ideas and details that are related to it. Now you must decide how you will present these ideas. Will you write about the most important ideas first? Are there events that happened in a particular order? Could you tell all the facts about how a subject looks, and then tell how it acts?

Use a Graphic Organizer

Graphic organizers are diagrams or charts that help you arrange your ideas in a logical way. Some examples are shown here. You can find many others on TIME FOR KIDS Homework Helper site: **www.timeforkids.com/hh/writeideas**

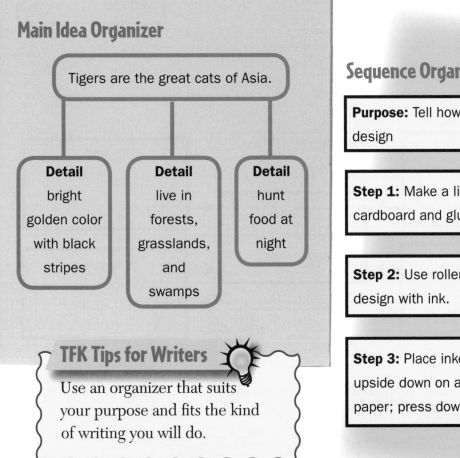

Main Idea Organizer

Tigers are the great cats of Asia.

Detail
bright golden color with black stripes

Detail
live in forests, grasslands, and swamps

Detail
hunt food at night

TFK Tips for Writers

Use an organizer that suits your purpose and fits the kind of writing you will do.

Sequence Organizer

Purpose: Tell how to print an original design

↓

Step 1: Make a line drawing on cardboard and glue string on lines.

↓

Step 2: Use roller to cover string design with ink.

↓

Step 3: Place inked string design upside down on a blank sheet of paper; press down and then remove.

More Graphic Organizers

Cause and Effect Diagram

Use a cause-and-effect diagram to plan a narrative or adventure story where one event triggers other events in the plot.

Cause

One January day, 13 inches of snow blanketed our town.

Effects

School was closed.

Dan and I shoveled the driveway.

All the kids in our neighborhood went sledding.

Try This!

Here is an organizer you could use to plan a personal narrative. This example shows a writer's plan for a narrative about an experience she had learning to water ski. How would you complete the organizer?

Experience Chart

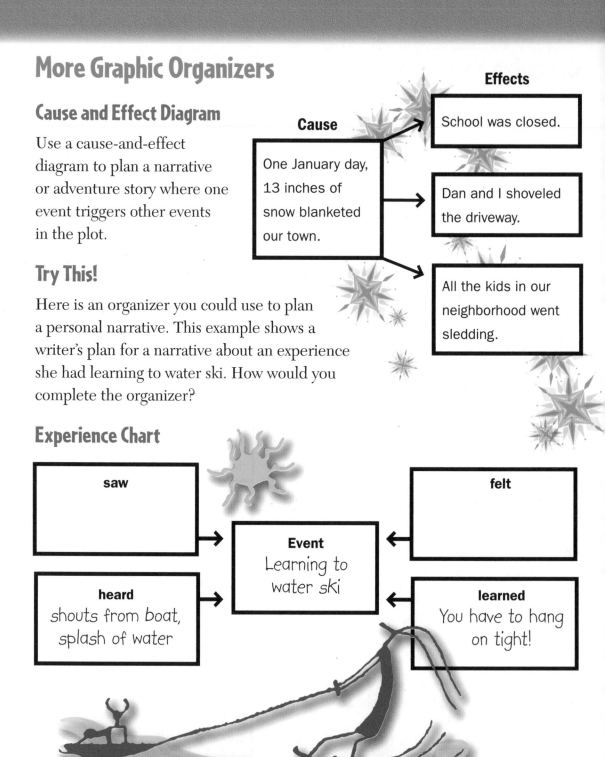

saw

felt

Event
Learning to water ski

heard
shouts from boat, splash of water

learned
You have to hang on tight!

Drafting

Time to write
a working draft,
or first copy

What Is a First Draft?

A first draft is your first attempt to write something. Your goal is to get all your ideas down on paper. If you get writer's block along the way, there are strategies you can use to keep going.

Tips from the Pros

The editors at TFK draft stories all the time. Here's what they say.

Jeremy Caplan: "First I write down the information that I know I will include in the story, like an important quote or some key facts. Then I figure out how those quotes and facts are linked together and add those linking sentences. I basically go step by step, piece by piece, adding to the story as if putting together a puzzle. Before long, the story writes itself!"

Nicole Iorio: "Sometimes I stop and read some more about whatever my topic is. Sometimes I just keep writing anything that comes into my head until I get to what I want to say. Sometimes I take a break and come back after I've taken a walk, gotten a drink of water, or listened to music."

A Sample First Draft

Attack!

The boy opens his eyes very slowly.

Add boy's name and age

(Suddenly a jolt rocks the small room.)

Make the year 2743

In a few weeks he will finally see his parents

again. It's been three years since they left him

with his grandmother and went to Mars to live

in an experimental (colny) of earthlings.

Caleb knows living on Mars may

be dangerous. Right now the shuttle

Explain why it's dangerous

is shaking badly.

The robot, Alywishus, (bersts) into

Add what the robot says

the room. He wants Caleb to follow him.

What Is Fiction?

Fiction is a kind of imaginary writing that has made-up characters and events. Narrative fiction includes myths, science fiction, historical fiction, adventure stories, and realistic stories about people just like you.

Myths and Legends

Myths and **legends** are fiction. They are stories that have been handed down through the years. Myths tell stories of gods or beings with superhuman powers. Often these tales attempt to explain something in nature. Legends are about heroes and their great deeds. Myths include stories about characters such as Pandora, Arachne, and Thor. The story of King Arthur is a legend.

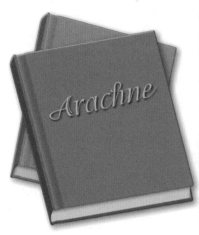

Try This!

Ask your teacher or librarian to help you find a myth or legend. Read the story and write the names of the main characters below. What makes this story a myth or legend?

_____

_____

_____

_____

Science Fiction

Science fiction stories combine science and fantasy. They often take place in the future or in another galaxy. Sometimes the author imagines technology that doesn't exist yet. Jules Verne's *Journey to the Center of the Earth* was one of the first science fiction books ever written.

Adventure Story

An **adventure story** tells about an exciting or unusual experience. Sometimes characters face dangerous situations and exhibit great courage. You may have read *The Adventures of Tom Sawyer* by Mark Twain or Gary Paulsen's *Hatchet*.

Try This!

Write the title of a science fiction or adventure story you know. What makes it exciting?

_____

_____

_____

TFK Tips for Fiction Writers

- Use your imagination.

- Think of a problem to solve.

- Describe when and where the events take place.

- Show what your characters are like by their words and actions.

Story Elements

Writing a story is like baking an apple pie. Just as the pie needs a crust, apples, and spices, a story needs certain ingredients. The ingredients in a story are the characters, setting, plot, and dialogue. We call these ingredients story elements.

Parts of a Story	
Characters	• The **characters** are the ones the story is about. Often they are people, but animals can also be characters in some types of stories.
Setting	• The **setting** is when and where the story takes place.
Plot	• The **plot** is what happens in the story. It centers on a problem and how the characters solve it.
Dialogue	• **Dialogue** is conversation between the characters. Their words show what they are thinking and feeling.

Time to Write

Look at a story you are writing. Does it describe the characters and setting? Does it tell what the problem is and how it is solved? Would dialogue add interest? Add any story elements that are missing.

TFK Tips for Writers

Including unexpected events or surprising twists in the plot will keep your readers in suspense and add interest to your story.

Creating Characters

Good stories have strong characters. Have you read about Meg Murry in *A Wrinkle in Time* or Harry Potter in one of J. K. Rowling's books? Then you know that interesting characters bring a story to life. They say and do things you remember.

The chart below shows how details can help make characters seem real.

Character Details	
How a character looks	Picture an 11-year-old boy who wears glasses and has a scar shaped like a lightning bolt on his forehead. That's Harry Potter.
How the character acts or feels	Harry feels left out because his classmates pick on him and he has to sleep in a closet under the stairs.
What the character does or likes to do	After Harry is invited to a special school, he discovers that he has a talent for Quidditch, a game played on flying brooms.

Time to Write

Look at a character from a story you are writing. Add details to describe the character more clearly and make the character seem more real.

The Attack is Back!

On page 24, you read part of a draft about Caleb. Look at how the writer has added details to develop the characters, plot, setting, and dialogue. Notice the spelling corrections and the improved order of two sentences.

Character

Attack!

Suddenly a jolt rocks the small room. Caleb opens his eyes very slowly and looks around. He doesn't know where he is at first. Suddenly he remembers. Today is his eleventh birthday. The year is 2743, and he's headed for Mars on the shuttle *Venture*.

Setting

In a few weeks he will finally see his parents again. It's been three years since they left him with his grandmother and traveled to Mars to live in an experimental colony of earthlings.

Plot

Caleb knows living on Mars may be dangerous. Warriors from Vasari are ready to take over the planet. Enemy assault ships have already attacked spaceships bringing people to the colony. All at once the shuttle shudders again, and the robot, Alywishus, bursts into the room.

"An assault ship is ramming us," he yells. "Let's hope the outer shields hold up. Come with me!"

Dialogue

Writing Dialogue

When you write a story, don't just tell what happens next. Use dialogue to show what the characters are thinking, feeling, and doing. Compare the statements below to the examples with dialogue. Which sentences help tell the story in a more lively, interesting way?

Michele tried hard when she played basketball.	"I would run inside crying," says Michele. "My mom would say, 'If you can't handle it, don't go back out there.' Then I'd go back out and try my hardest to beat them."
The explosion scared Laura.	"It was frightening. I'd never been close to a bomb before," said Laura. "I thought the school might get bombed next."
The firefighter told us to leave.	"Put on your coats, please," he said. "Turn off anything on your stove. You need to leave the building immediately."

Try This!

On a separate sheet of paper, write a brief dialogue that shows how a character feels about a special event that is taking place.

Time to Write

Look at a story you are writing. Ask yourself the questions on the checklist. Add details to your story so that you can answer "yes" to each question.

Checklist for a Story

- ☐ Did I start with a good idea?
- ☐ Did I tell where and when my story takes place?
- ☐ Did I use exact words to create a strong main character?
- ☐ Did I present a problem to solve?
- ☐ Did I include dialogue that moves the plot along?
- ☐ Did I tell the story events in order?
- ☐ Did I make sure each sentence makes sense?

What Is Nonfiction?

Nonfiction is writing about real events and real people. It includes interviews, how-to articles, essays, and letters. Narrative nonfiction tells a story. Personal narratives about your own experiences and biographies about other people are two kinds of narrative nonfiction.

Personal Narrative

A **personal narrative** tells a true story about something that happened to you. The paragraph below is the beginning of a narrative that tells about the author's experience in gym class one day. Do the title and opening make you want to read more? Why do you think so?

Keep an Eye on the Sky!

I was in gym class when my teacher suggested we go outside and play softball. As we made our way out to the field, my stomach slowly turned into a giant knot of fear.

TFK Tips for Writers

Follow these steps when you write a personal narrative.

- Write about an experience you had.
- Grab the reader's attention with a strong opening.
- Tell the events in order. Give details to help the reader visualize what you are describing.
- Let readers hear your voice. Express your thoughts and feelings in a way that sounds like you.

How-to Article

A **how-to article** explains how to do or make something. Begin a how-to article by telling readers what activity you will be explaining. Then list the materials needed to do the activity. Finally, use time-order organization to tell the steps they must follow. Some clue words that show time order are *first*, *next*, *then*, and *finally*.

The paragraph below is part of an article about making sun prints. The boldface words and phrases help tell the sequence, or order, of the steps. What other time-order words can you think of?

> **First,** gather the materials you will need. **Then** go outside and place one piece of light-sensitive paper on the ground with the blue side facing up. **Next,** place your small objects on top of the paper. Work fast! Leave the paper and objects out in the sun for two to four minutes. The paper will turn white. **After that happens,** remove the objects and place the paper in the bowl of water. Soak the paper for two minutes. **Finally,** take the paper out of the water and place it on a flat surface. As it dries, the paper will darken, and you will have a print made by the sun.

TFK Tips for Writers

Follow these steps when you write nonfiction.
- Choose a topic.
- Decide on a purpose—to inform, persuade, teach, or entertain.
- Check your facts.
- Keep your audience in mind.
- Use time-order words to show steps in sequence.

Time to Write

Look at a personal narrative, how-to article, or other piece of nonfiction that you are writing. Which tip could you try?

Finding Information

Good nonfiction writing includes exact words and accurate information. You can use a variety of resources to gather data and check your facts. The kind of information you need will help you determine the best reference works to use.

- Use a **dictionary** to find word meanings and check spelling.

- Check a **thesaurus** to find synonyms and antonyms that add variety to your writing.

- Choose an **encyclopedia** to find articles that offer information on a wide variety of topics.

- Use an **almanac** to find statistics such as the population of a city or the elevation of a mountain.

- Read **nonfiction books** to find more detailed information about a certain topic.

- Look on the **Internet** to find up-to-date facts about many different subjects.

TFK Tips for Writers

When you write an article or report,
- use at least two different sources of information.
- take good notes on the information you find. Use index cards or a notebook.

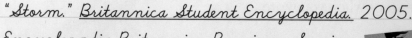

"Storm." *Britannica Student Encyclopedia.* 2005.
Encyclopædia Britannica Premium Service
Hurricane
- has wind speed of more than 75 mph
- forms over ocean and moves across
  warm water
- produces downpours
- weakens after moving inland

Including Main Ideas and Supporting Details

Every article or report that you write should have a topic, or subject. Sentences are organized into paragraphs that tell something about that subject. Each paragraph has a **topic sentence** that states the **main idea,** or what the paragraph is mostly about. The other sentences give **supporting details** that provide further information about the main idea. Read the paragraph below from a report on hurricanes.

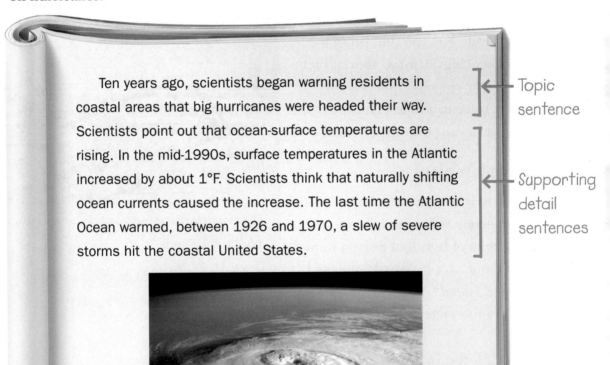

Ten years ago, scientists began warning residents in coastal areas that big hurricanes were headed their way. ← Topic sentence

Scientists point out that ocean-surface temperatures are rising. In the mid-1990s, surface temperatures in the Atlantic increased by about 1°F. Scientists think that naturally shifting ocean currents caused the increase. The last time the Atlantic Ocean warmed, between 1926 and 1970, a slew of severe storms hit the coastal United States. ← Supporting detail sentences

Tip from a Pro

Dina el Nabli, TFK Senior Content Producer, says: "While doing research, I determine the most important and interesting piece of information in the story. If I think it will also be 'new news' to readers, it usually ends up being the main idea."

Fact or Opinion?

Presenting accurate facts is especially important when you are writing an article, essay, or other forms of nonfiction. Including precise facts will give your readers a true picture of the topic you are writing about. When you avoid errors, your readers know that they can count on your writing for correct information.

What Is a Fact?

Facts are pieces of information that can be proved. You can find proof for facts by checking a trusted source such as a good encyclopedia or a reliable Web site. You can also ask an expert or write from your own experience.

What Is an Opinion?

An **opinion** is one person's belief. When someone states an opinion, it is an expression of how that person thinks or feels about a topic. Words such as *I think, I feel, should, best,* and *most* are often clues to a statement of opinion.

Fact: Hurricane Charley struck Florida's west coast on August 13, 2004.

Opinion: Hurricanes are the worst kind of storm there is.

Opinion: The federal government should do more to help hurricane victims.

Can You Tell the Difference?

Read the following sentences. Write **F** on the line in front of each fact and write **O** in front of each opinion. Which statements would you probably include in a report?

_____ Giraffes are the most amazing animals in the world.

_____ These tall creatures live on grasslands in Africa.

_____ They can gallop up to 35 miles per hour.

_____ Everyone should visit Africa to see the giraffes.

Try This!

Read the paragraph below. Draw a line under three facts. Circle the two sentences that illustrate opinions. How could you check your answers?

A Flurry of Hurricanes

Florida seems like a really dangerous place to live. Ivan was the third hurricane to pound the state during August and September of 2004. Hurricane Charley struck Florida's west coast on August 13, 2004. On September 5, hurricane Frances made landfall on the east coast of Florida. Then, just three weeks later, Jeanne struck Florida. "Scientists expected an especially stormy season," says Stanley Goldenberg, a research meteorologist in Miami, Florida. "I'm in shock over the damage and the deaths, but I am not surprised," he told TIME.

Time to Write

Look at a report or other piece of nonfiction that you are writing. Underline the facts. Check them in a resource you trust. Find one opinion and replace it with a fact.

Underline the facts.

TFK Tips for Writers

When you quote someone who is an expert on a certain topic, be sure to include the person's exact words. That way the information you provide for your readers will be accurate.

Essay

An **essay** is a short piece of writing on a particular topic. It may be serious or humorous. The purpose can be to persuade, to entertain, or to inform. Some essays might relate an experience the writer has had or describe a certain person, place, or event.

Organize an essay in a way that fits your purpose. You might write an essay to

- compare and contrast two similar things.
- describe a scene or an object.
- show a cause-and-effect relationship.
- present a problem and solution.

The following piece was written to bring attention to a problem with animals that are taken from their natural habitats and sold as pets. Note that the problem is identified and explained at the beginning of the essay. What solution does the writer suggest in the conclusion?

For Sale: Stolen Rare Pets

All over the world, rare birds, reptiles, and monkeys are stolen from their jungle homes and sneaked into pet markets. This illegal business is called animal smuggling. It is big business. It's worth billions of dollars a year.

How do rare animals get to pet shops? First, they are stolen from the wild by poor villagers who know just where to look for a baby monkey or a wild bird. Smugglers often pay only a few dollars for such animals. Then they are taken out of the country to places where they are sold for a high price.

The U.S. is working with other countries to stop the smuggling. In 1998 a man said to be one of the world's biggest reptile traders was arrested. But the best way to stop smuggling is this: Don't buy an endangered animal!

Organizing Ideas

Good writers use **transitions** to move from one paragraph to the next in an essay and to organize their ideas within a paragraph. Transitions are words or phrases that link ideas together. There are various kinds of transitions. Consider the examples below.

Cause and Effect	because, since, as a result, so that, therefore
Compare and Contrast	similarly, however, although, in contrast
Additional Ideas	also, too, in addition
Time Order	before, after, first, next, finally

The paragraphs below are from an essay about a decision to bring wolves back to Yellowstone National Park. Use the boldface transitions to help you identify which ideas are causes and which are effects.

The Wolf Packs are Back

For centuries, packs of wolves roamed the West. But when white settlers came in the 1800s, they feared wolves **because** wolves often killed the sheep and cattle.

Since the government wanted to help the farmers, it paid hunters to kill wolves. By the early 1930s, all of Yellowstone's wolves were gone. Coyotes and elk, which are hunted by wolves, grew in numbers. **As a result,** plants that are eaten by elk began to disappear. **Therefore,** the government decided to bring wolves back to Yellowstone.

Try This!

Read these sentences. Identify the transitions and explain how they help link the writer's ideas.

- Rick set the table in addition to practicing the trumpet and finishing his homework.
- Hurricanes form over warm ocean waters. In contrast, tornadoes form over land.
- Put on your helmet before riding a bike.

Time to Write

Read a draft you have written. Look for places where adding a transition would make your meaning clearer or improve the flow of the sentences.

TFK Tips for Writers

When you write an essay, include an introduction, a middle section with details, and a conclusion. Use a checklist to review your draft before revising.

Checklist for Nonfiction

☐ I wrote an introduction that grabs the reader's attention.

☐ I included a topic sentence and supporting details.

☐ I organized my sentences in an order that makes sense.

☐ I used transitions to link my ideas.

☐ I used reliable sources to check facts.

☐ I wrote so that readers can hear my voice.

☐ I checked my writing for errors in capitalization, punctuation, and spelling.

Interview

When you conduct an **interview,** you talk with someone to get information. Later you write about the ideas and viewpoints expressed by the person you spoke with. Interviews are often published in newspapers and magazines.

It is important to prepare beforehand for an interview. One of the best ways to get ready is to think about what kind of information you want to obtain. Is the person you are interviewing an expert on a certain subject? Has he or she had a unique experience that would be interesting to others? Once you've decided what it is you want to find out, write some questions that will get the person talking about that topic.

A Scoop from Annie

Below is the introduction and one of the questions from an interview conducted by TFK reporter Annie Vernick.

I recently visited bestselling author and illustrator Chris Van Allsburg in his Providence, Rhode Island, home to discuss the movie based on his book *The Polar Express.*

Sitting in his art-filled living room, I saw lots of things that reminded me of his 15 picture books: a huge model sailboat, an old-fashioned broom, fanciful toy animals, a robot figure, and a model steam engine. Read on to find out what I learned from the man behind the amazing tales.

TFK: In the movie, the conductor says: "It doesn't matter where the train is going. What matters is deciding to get on." Does this mean it's not important to have a destination?

Van Allsburg: I think it means it's important to commit yourself to pursuing something, to trying something, to the possibility that miracles can happen.

Try This!

The paragraph below was based on an interview the writer conducted with an amazing ten-year-old. What questions did the writer probably ask? After reading the paragraph, complete the web to show information the interviewer gathered for the story.

Most little kids are happy to watch cartoons. Not Robert V. J. Gupta. When he was three years old, he would switch the TV channel to classical music concerts. Why? "I thought they were more amusing!" he says. At age three, he also began to play the violin. Now ten, Robert delights audiences with concerts of his own. He plays with orchestras at such famous places as New York City's Carnegie Hall. Next month Robert will perform in India, his parents' homeland. "The violin is a wonderful instrument," he says. "It has brought me so many places."

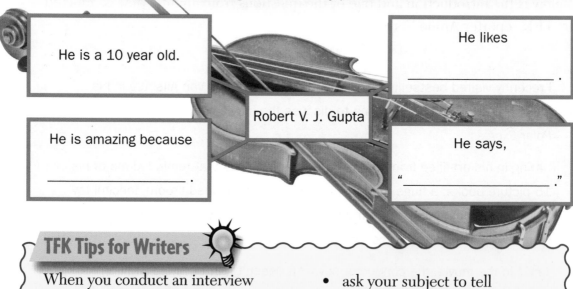

He is a 10 year old.

He likes

_____ .

Robert V. J. Gupta

He is amazing because

_____ .

He says,

"_____ ."

Time to Write

Interview a classmate. Before you meet, consider what you want to say about your subject and write questions that will help you get the information you need. Take good notes during the interview. Then write a paragraph. Tell what makes your classmate special!

Questions for my interview.

Interview Checklist

☐ I prepared ahead of time.

☐ I took good notes.

☐ I chose words carefully to describe the person or event.

☐ I told why this person is important.

☐ I checked my writing for misspelled words.

☐ I checked to make sure I capitalized names of people and places.

☐ I used quotation marks for the person's exact words.

☐ I wrote neatly.

Tip from a Pro

Jennifer Marino, Staff Writer for TFK, says: "The tricky part about interviewing someone is making sure you do your homework beforehand. Conduct research on the person, find out why they are important, and come prepared with questions that can't be answered with a simple yes or no."

Writing to Persuade

When you write to **persuade,** you share your views on an issue that is important to you. Your purpose is to convince others that your way of thinking makes sense. Your writing should support your opinion with strong reasons, facts, and examples. Persuasive writing often suggests an action that readers might take.

Writing to persuade can take many forms, such as a letter, an editorial, or a speech. Choose a kind of writing that is suited to your audience and your message.

Read the letter below. What is the topic? What does the writer want someone to do? What conclusion should the reader draw?

Dear Mr. President,

    Bang! Bang! This is the sound of another innocent person getting hurt or killed with a gun. This tragic event affects many people. It must be stopped. Violence involving guns is a major problem in our country. — Topic sentence
If no one stops it, more and more people will be injured.

    How can we stop it? My idea is to make guns a lot harder to buy. First of all, some guns that can hurt very seriously should be outlawed. Guns that can be sold should have higher prices, so cost would be a — Supporting Arguments
problem. Much more paperwork would have to be signed. Those who have a criminal record should not be able to buy a gun.

    I truly believe this issue is most important to all Americans, including kids. I think we all want a safer America. — Conclusion

Sincerely,
Beth Keyes

Time to Write

What do you think about the right to own firearms? Write you own persuasive letter expressing your point of view.

Organize Your Ideas

Think about your topic. Think about your own opinion and the reasons why you feel that way. Consider how you would respond to other points of view.

At the beginning of your essay, tell different viewpoints on the issue and then explain your own point of view. Include your reasons, and provide facts and examples to support them. Conclude by restating your opinion and the reasons why people should take action.

A writer created the organizer below to write a persuasive essay about an important environmental issue. Identify the issue and explain the different viewpoints.

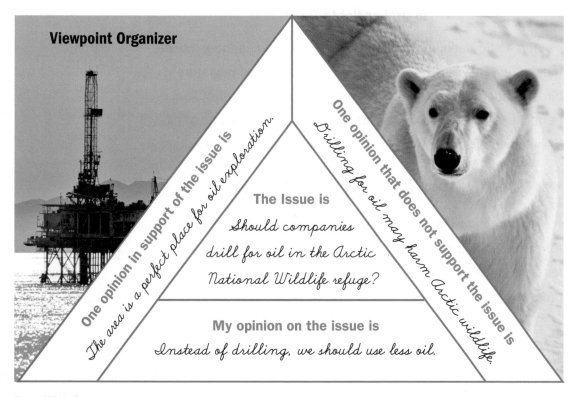

Viewpoint Organizer

One opinion in support of the issue is *The area is a perfect place for oil exploration.*

One opinion that does not support the issue is *Drilling for oil may harm Arctic wildlife.*

The Issue is
Should companies drill for oil in the Arctic National Wildlife refuge?

My opinion on the issue is
Instead of drilling, we should use less oil.

Try This!

Use a triangle organizer to sort out the different viewpoints about an issue that is important to you. Write the topic in the middle triangle and state your opinion on the issue. Complete the sentences on each side to show opposing viewpoints.

Be Convincing

When you write to persuade, voice your opinion with enthusiasm. Think about your audience and decide on the best way to share your message. Whom do you want to persuade? What action do you want others to take? Will you write a letter? give a speech?

Here are the first and last paragraphs from a persuasive essay. Note that in the first paragraph the writer points out arguments on both sides of the issue. In the conclusion, the writer clearly states her opinion and suggests an action that supports this point of view.

To Drill or Not to Drill?

The Arctic National Wildlife Refuge is home to caribou, moose, musk oxen, wolves, foxes, grizzlies, polar bears, and migratory birds. Leaders in the oil industry believe the refuge is the perfect site for the "environmentally sensitive exploration" of oil. Environmentalists are wondering: What will become of the wildlife?

Writer gives opposing viewpoints to summarize the issue.

Americans are the largest consumers of oil. Instead of drilling for oil, we should decrease our need for foreign oil simply by using less. We must all work together to cut back on the oil we use in order to preserve the wildlife of the Arctic National Wildlife Refuge.

Writer suggests solution and appeals to the reader to help.

TFK Tips for Writers

Think of the final ideas of a persuasive piece as "gotcha" sentences. Imagine what you would say to make your point in an argument. Use this as a clincher to convince your readers to agree with your views and take action.

Try This!

Write an opening paragraph for a persuasive piece on an issue you care about.
Be sure to present both sides of the issue before stating your opinion. Write
about one of these topics, or another that you choose.

The Environment	**Keeping Pets on Leashes**
Saving Wildlife	**Litterbugs**

Time to Write

Look at a letter, editorial, or speech that you are
writing. Then ask yourself each question on the list.

Checklist for Writing to Persuade

- ☐ Did I state my opinion on the topic clearly?

- ☐ Did I include at least two strong reasons to support my opinion?

- ☐ Did I conclude by telling what action I think my readers should take?

- ☐ Did I keep focused on the topic?

- ☐ Did I use a variety of sentence lengths— some short and some long?

- ☐ Did I let readers hear my voice?

- ☐ Did I use a new paragraph for each different idea?

TFK Tips for Writers

- Choose an issue you really care about.
- Make sure you have enough strong reasons to support your opinion.
- Conclude by restating your opinion.
- Tell your audience what action you'd like them to take.

Strong Openings and Closings

Draw Your Readers In

The opening of a story is sometimes called a "lead." The lead can be a single sentence, or it can be one or more paragraphs. A **strong opening** creates interest right away and leads your audience into the story or article. It grabs the readers' attention and entices them to continue reading. Good writers use a variety of leads to draw readers into stories. Here are a few examples from TIME FOR KIDS stories.

The Unexpected	Many American kids starting back to school this fall missed something important: a classroom!
A Question	How does it feel to lose a billion dollars and ten years of hard work? NASA scientists know all too well.
A Strong Visual Image	Elizabeth Eckford felt the first wet splotch of spit hit her skin. She held her head high.
A Compelling Description	In the dark night of Southern India, the wind carried an unmistakable sound: a lone woman was crying.

Try This!

Which of the leads above do you think is most interesting? Why? Use one of these methods to write a strong lead for an article or story about one of the following topics or about another topic that interests you.

- the importance of eating nutritious foods
- an experience you had last summer
- a description of a pet or favorite animal

_____

_____

Write a Strong Closing

Strong Closing

Any article or story you write should end with a **strong closing,** or conclusion, that gives your work a finished feeling. A closing should sum up the main points of an article or tell the outcome of a story.

When you write about an opinion, close with convincing statements that clinch your argument and encourage your readers to take action. Look at two possible endings for a persuasive essay on protecting our forests. Which closing do you think is more effective in accomplishing its purpose? Why?

Weak Closing	Strong Closing
Trees shouldn't be cut down.	Trees provide lumber, shade, and an ecological balance for the environment. We must protect our forests so that one hundred years from now, people will still enjoy this valuable resource.

Try This!

Here's a weak closing for a paragraph about a favorite activity of the writer. Use what you have learned to improve this closing. You may write the closing for a paragraph about a sport, hobby, or other activity that you enjoy.

Weak Closing: And that's why I play this sport.

Time to Write

Look at a piece of your own writing. Analyze your opening and closing. Are they weak or strong? What changes could you make to improve them?

A poem is a piece of writing in which a writer uses words to express ideas in a fun or imaginative way. Poets often focus on the sounds of language, choosing words that rhyme or grouping words with repeated sounds.

Limericks

A **limerick** is a humorous 5-line verse that has a particular rhyming pattern and rhythm.

- Lines 1, 2, and 5 rhyme;
  each line has three beats.

- Lines 3 and 4 rhyme;
  each line has two beats.

> There was a Young Lady whose chin,
> Resembled the point of a pin:
> So she had it made sharp,
> And purchased a harp,
> And played several tunes with her chin.

Listen for the rhythm and rhyming words as you read aloud this limerick by Edward Lear.

Time to Write

Add words to complete the limerick below. You may need to change some of the words to fit your ideas.

There was a _____ whose _____

Looked just like _____

So _____

And _____

And played _____

Concrete Poems

When creating poems, writers arrange words in ways that have interesting rhythms. Often they use sound patterns such as rhyme or alliteration—a series of several words beginning with the same sound. Poets use a few vibrant words to paint a picture in the reader's imagination.

Like other poetry, **concrete poems** focus on the sounds of language. However, they also appeal to the reader's visual sense. The words of the poem are arranged in a shape that resembles the subject. Read the poem about a butterfly below. How does the shape of the poem work together with the words to create an image and feeling of this creature?

Gentle breezes whisper

Fragile wings flutter

silently light

on delicate petals

To sip sweet nectar

Time to Write

Create your own concrete poem. Brainstorm a list of vivid verbs, adjectives, and adverbs that will help readers visualize your subject. Arrange words and phrases to show the shape of the thing you are writing about.

Cinquains

A **cinquain** is a brief, five-line poem with a definite pattern. The writer paints a picture using a few well-chosen words that describe the subject of the poem. Listen to the rhythm of the words in this cinquain.

Copperhead
Poisonous, treacherous
Slithering, hissing, attacking
Beware the pit viper
SNAKE

When you write a cinquain, start by choosing an interesting subject. Then arrange words using the following pattern:

- Line 1: one word that names the subject of the poem.
- Line 2: two adjectives that describe the subject
- Line 3: three action words (usually with *-ing* endings) that tell what the subject does
- Line 4: a four-word phrase about the subject or a feeling related to it
- Line 5: one word that is a synonym for the opening word

Try This!

Write a cinquain like the example on this page. Use one of the words below as the subject of your poem, or think of one on your own.

Sisters   Frog   Puppy   Dentist

_____

_____

_____

_____

_____

TFK Tips for Poetry Writers

- Use your imagination. Arrange your words to express an idea or feeling.
- Make every word count. Replace wordy phrases such as *moves along the ground* with vivid verbs such as *slithers*.
- Pay attention to rhythm and rhyme. Read your poem aloud and listen to the flow of the words.

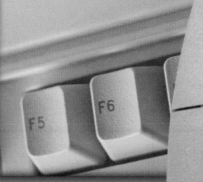

3

Revising

Time to make changes
to improve your draft

Time to Revise

Good writers reflect on, or think about, what they have written. Often they share their writing with others. They listen to suggestions for how they can express their ideas more clearly and make their writing more interesting.

Smooth, Smoother, Smoothest!

When you revise, look for sentences that flow smoothly. They are easy to read and understand. How can you make your writing smooth? One strategy is to break apart sentences that are too long. Another is to use phrases and connecting words to combine short, choppy sentences. Writers also vary the rhythm of their writing by turning some statements into questions or exclamations.

First Draft	Kids can't wear jeans and T-shirts to school anymore and the cost of a uniform is about $100 and it is cheaper than buying several different outfits. Not everyone is happy. Not everyone likes uniforms.
Revised	Goodbye baggy jeans and tie-dyed T-shirts! Although the cost of a uniform is about $100, it is cheaper than buying several different outfits. Yet, not everyone is happy about the idea of wearing uniforms.

Try This!

Reread the revised paragraph. Which stringy sentence did the writer break up? How were transition words used to link ideas? Which sentence adds a light, humorous touch to the paragraph?

Time to Revise

Read your first draft aloud to a partner and listen to the way the sentences flow. Ask these questions.

- Is my writing clear?
- Will my audience be interested?
- Does it sound as if I am speaking?

Time to Write a Title

A good title hints at the topic. It also creates a feeling of suspense that makes readers want to know what happens.

TFK reporter **Joe McGowan** says, "I start with a title. It often changes, but it forces me to start someplace."

Here are titles of some popular books. How do they grab a reader's attention?

- *Shadow Spinner*
- *A Year Down Yonder*
- *The Slippery Slope*

Read the titles on the book covers below. Which makes you want to pick up the book and start reading? How could you improve the others? Jot down your ideas!

The City • The Cat and the Mouse • The Curious Encounter on Bay Drive • One Day

Time to Write a Title

Look at something you are writing. Give it a title that tells about the topic and creates interest for your readers.

My Fabulous Fortune

TFK Tips for Writers

- Use words that begin with the same sound.
- Give a clue to your topic.
- Revise your title if your story takes a new direction.

Time to Write a Beginning

Begin with a sentence that creates interest and gives a little information about the topic. The beginning is important in both fiction and nonfiction. A strong opening makes the reader decide, "Yes, I want to read this!"

Begin with a question	Which countries crank out the most trash? Unfortunately, the U.S. is on top of the heap.
Begin with a quotation	"Stop, kid! Get off that bike!" Kids in Florida who ride a bicycle without wearing a helmet could hear those words from the police.
Begin with a description	The howling winds and the sheets of rain came first. Palm trees pounded by wind and water bent over and touched the ground.

Try This!

How would you revise these opening sentences to make your audience want to continue reading?

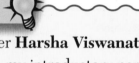

Tip from a Pro

TFK Kid Reporter **Harsha Viswanathan** says, "I generally begin my introductory paragraph with a hook—either an interesting quote, an anecdote, a question, or a startling statistic."

A girl lives next door.

_____

Cats make good pets.

_____

Abraham Lincoln was a president.

_____

Openings That Hook Readers

Here are some more examples of good opening sentences:

> According to Coast Guard Officer Jackson Powers, the huge glacier is "a serious threat to both penguins and ships in the area."

> "Eeeek!" The ear-piercing shriek came from somewhere down the hall.

> Can you imagine raising $20,000 in just one week?

Great Beginnings in Books

Here are the openings of two great books. What characters are introduced? Do you want to read more of either or both books? Why or why not?

We called him Old Yeller. The name had a sort of double meaning. One part meant that his short hair was a dingy yellow, a color that we called "yeller" in those days. The other meant that when he opened his head, the sound he let out came closer to being a yell than a bark.

— from *Old Yeller* by Fred Gipson

"Tom!"

No answer.

"Tom!"

No answer.

"What's gone with that boy, I wonder? You Tom!"

— from *The Adventures of Tom Sawyer* by Mark Twain

Time to Revise

Look at something you are revising. Does it have a strong beginning that will make readers want to keep reading?

Time to Make the Meaning Clear

When you revise your writing, check to be sure that the ideas or events are ordered in a way that will make sense to your readers.

Putting Ideas in Order

Read the paragraphs below. Look for clues to determine the beginning, middle, and end of the story. Then number the sentences and reread them in order to tell the story.

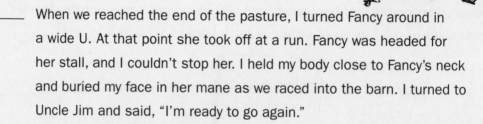

_____ When we reached the end of the pasture, I turned Fancy around in a wide U. At that point she took off at a run. Fancy was headed for her stall, and I couldn't stop her. I held my body close to Fancy's neck and buried my face in her mane as we raced into the barn. I turned to Uncle Jim and said, "I'm ready to go again."

_____ Today, at long last, I get to ride Uncle Jim's horse, Fancy, all by myself! This morning I brushed Fancy as usual. Then I watched as Uncle Jim saddled her. He picked me up and put me in the saddle, and we walked to the pasture.

_____ I was excited and nervous. I pressed the left rein across Fancy's neck, turning her head to the right. Then I put my heels to her ribs. She turned right and headed just as I wanted. Before I knew it, we were going fast along the fence.

Time Order Words

Good writers use **transitions,** clue words that help to organize their writing. Did you notice the words _today, this morning,_ and _then_ in the personal narrative above? These are clues for time order. Other words such as _first, next, before,_ and _finally_ also tell the order of events in a story.

Adding Details

As you revise a piece you have written, look for places to add details that will make your writing more interesting. Use words and phrases that help readers picture objects and events you describe. Good writers create vivid scenes so their audience can easily imagine the setting, characters, and action in a story.

The following paragraphs were taken from a narrative about Ty Murray, a champion rodeo cowboy. How do descriptive words and phrases add interest for readers?

Ty Murray takes on the **roughest, toughest** opponents in sports. Each opponent is **an explosive bundle of energy** that could flatten an NFL defensive line **without breaking a sweat.**

Who are these **awesome** athletes? They're **gut-busting, bucking** horses and **whirling, snorting** bulls **with bad attitudes.**

Ty is **strong, flexible,** and **graceful.** Bullriding is his specialty. He rides a bull **as if he were glued to its back.** When a ride is over, **he lands on the ground as softly as a cat landing on a pillow.**

Try This!

Choose one of the sentences below or write one of your own. Add descriptive words and phrases that will help readers visualize the scene.

A pony trotted.

Clouds gathered.

Athletes practice.

The orchestra played music.

Time to Revise

With a partner, read over something you have written. Try to answer these questions.

- Does the order of facts and ideas make sense?
- Are there places where adding time order words would make the meaning clearer?
- Would adding details help readers visualize the characters or action in the story?

Time to Put Words in Order

When you write your first draft, you write quickly. Your words may not be arranged in the best order. When you revise, change the order of the words to say what you really mean.

Putting words in the wrong order can be confusing. Compare the two sentences below. What changes made the meaning clearer?

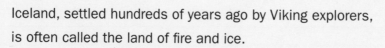

> Iceland, settled hundreds of years ago by Viking explorers, is often called the land of fire and ice.
>
> Settled hundreds of years ago by Viking explorers, Iceland is often called the land of fire and ice.

Placing related ideas near each other in a sentence will help readers understand the meaning. Why does the revised sentence below make more sense than the first draft?

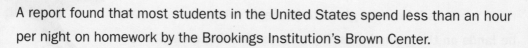

> A report found that most students in the United States spend less than an hour per night on homework by the Brookings Institution's Brown Center.
>
> A report by the Brookings Institution's Brown Center found that most students in the United States spend less than an hour per night on homework.

Try This!

How would you change these sentences to make them easier to read? Draw circles and arrows. There may be more than one way to revise a sentence!

Fishing and mining in Iceland are more important than farming.

The sixth-grade student has transferred to another school with red hair and sparkling blue eyes.

Time to Choose Strong Nouns

Nouns are words that name persons, places, things, and ideas. Strong, exact nouns express precise ideas. They help readers understand and visualize the writer's ideas. Compare the two sentences below. Which one helps you picture more clearly what the writer is trying to express?

> **People** use an **instrument** to observe **things**.
>
> **Astronomers** use a **telescope** to observe **planets** and **stars**.

When you revise, replace weak, general nouns with words that convey exact meaning. Your writing will be more interesting and will accomplish your purpose more effectively.

Try This!

Add to each list of exact nouns.

Persons	Places	Things or Ideas
astronomer	universe	shuttle
sister	museum	freedom
_____	_____	_____
_____	_____	_____

Time to Revise

Look at a piece of your own writing. Replace dull, general nouns with strong, interesting words with more exact meanings. Warm up by revising the brief passage below.

> Some **people** traveled to the **city** on vacation. They visited a **building.** Everyone ate **food** at a **place** near the park.

Time to Use Vivid Verbs

Verbs are words that tell the action in a sentence. Strong verbs help readers visualize exactly what is happening. You can use colorful action words to add pizzazz to your writing.

Choose a Good Action Word

Dull Verb	Improved	Even Better
went	ran	dashed

Compare the different pictures created in your mind by verbs that have meanings similar to *ran*.

Wild horses **galloped** through the canyon.

The toddlers **scampered** across the playground.

Mr. McCasney **sprinted** toward the plane.

Use Active Voice Verbs

Good writers use the active voice. This means that the subject is doing the acting. In the passive voice, the subject is being acted upon. Here is an example:

- **Active Voice:** The Wildcats defeated us.
- **Passive Voice:** We were defeated by the Wildcats.

How would you revise this passive voice sentence to put it in the active voice?

The project was completed by the class in the fall.

Try It!

Replace the verbs in red type with more vivid verbs. Read aloud the revised sentences.

Two friends **walked** along a mountain trail. A deer **moved** through the woods ahead of them.

A hawk **flew** overhead.

TFK Tips for Writers

Use a Thesaurus to find more exact nouns and verbs. It lists synonyms, words with similar meanings, for words you may want to replace.

Time to Add Adjectives

Writers use **adjectives** to help readers see, hear, taste, smell, and feel what they are describing.

> **Adjectives** are words that modify, or tell more about, nouns and pronouns. They tell *what kind, which one,* or *how many* about nouns.

sleek, black cat

Try This!

Look at the paragraph below. Notice the words in red. How do they help you see, hear, smell, taste, or feel the squid? Reread the sentences without the words in red. Can you tell the difference?

"It is **still** and **wet** and in a **giant** metal case. On the case, someone scratched the letters S-Q-U-I-D-Z-I-L-L-A. It's a **giant** squid, one of the earth's most **mysterious** animals."

three sweet ripe melons

Time to Revise

Reread a piece you have written. Add some colorful, strong adjectives to improve your writing. Warm up by adding at least two adjectives to each noun in the list.

1 _____	tomato	6 _____	tree
2 _____	book	7 _____	jacket
3 _____	lizard	8 _____	truck
4 _____	friend	9 _____	feeling
5 _____	song	10 _____	rain

Time to Add Adverbs

Good writers use **adverbs** to help readers visualize action.

> **Adverbs** modify, or tell more about, verbs. They tell how, when, or where an action takes place. Adverbs can also modify adjectives or other adverbs.

> **Tip from TFK Kid Reporter Mustafa Saifuddin:**
> "I try to be very specific and use adjectives, adverbs, and verbs that will come alive in readers' imaginations."

Try This!

Look at the paragraph below. Notice the adverbs in red. What does each one tell about another word?

Crows are **very** intelligent birds. They learn **easily** and have been taught to imitate human speech. After **aggressively** taking food from a picnic table or a coin from the ground, they **often** hide their treasure **somewhere.**

Time to Revise

Look at something you have written. Add adverbs to make your writing more interesting. Warm up by adding adverbs to tell how, when, or where. Work with a partner and compare the adverbs you have chosen.

1 walk _____

2 ask _____

3 exercise _____

4 cry _____

5 behave _____

6 paint _____

7 study _____

8 knock _____

The giant cat leaps very quickly. It always stalks its prey patiently.

The lion roars loudly.

4

Editing and Proofreading

Time to find and fix any mistakes

Writing Great Sentences

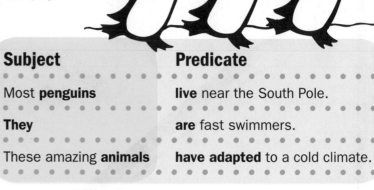

Sentences are the foundation of good writing. A **sentence** is a group of words that expresses a complete thought. Each sentence has two parts—a **subject** and a **predicate.** The

Subject	Predicate
Most **penguins**	**live** near the South Pole.
They	**are** fast swimmers.
These amazing **animals**	**have adapted** to a cold climate.

subject tells whom or what the sentence is about. The main word in the subject is always a noun or a pronoun. The **predicate** tells what the subject is or does. The verb is always the main word in a predicate.

Two subjects or two predicates can be joined with connecting words, such as *and.* These are called **compound subjects** and **compound predicates.**

Compound Subject	Compound Predicate
Sam **and** Josh	mowed the lawn **and** swept the porch.

Sometimes the subject or predicate is missing from a group of words. This incomplete thought is called a **sentence fragment.** What words could you add to make each of these fragments a sentence?

The frisky puppy _____

_____ disagreed about which movie to go see.

Time to Edit

Look back at a piece of writing you are editing. Does each sentence have a subject and a predicate? Add words to any sentence fragments to make complete sentences.

TFK Tips for Writers

To avoid sentence fragments, express your ideas in complete sentences that include a subject and predicate.

A Sentence for Every Reason

Writers use different kinds of sentences to accomplish their goals. Using a variety of sentences adds interest to your writing.

Kinds of Sentences

- A **declarative sentence** makes a statement. It ends with a period.
  Sacramento is the capital of California.

- An **imperative sentence** makes a command or request. It ends with a period.
  Show me Sacramento on the map.

- An **interrogative sentence** asks a question. It ends with a question mark.
  Where is Sacramento?

- An **exclamatory sentence** expresses a strong feeling, such as surprise, fear, or excitement. It ends with an exclamation point.
  I had the best visit to Sacramento!

> The subject of an imperative sentence is always *you*. This is called the "understood" subject.
>
> (You) Finish your homework.

When two or more ideas are strung together without any punctuation, the result is a **stringy sentence.** You can break up stringy sentences by putting each idea in a shorter sentence or by grouping related ideas in separate sentences with correct punctuation.

Polar bears are excellent swimmers and they often swim through icy water and thick fur and a layer of blubber keep them warm.

Polar bears are excellent swimmers. They often swim through icy water, **but** thick fur and a layer of blubber keep them warm.

67

Try This!

Tell how you would break up this stringy sentence from a report on nutrition.

> Choosing good foods helps people stay healthy and vegetables are full of vitamins and dairy products have calcium for strong bones and teeth.

Time to Edit

Read aloud a piece of writing that you are editing. Does the punctuation mark at the end of each sentence match the sound of your voice as you read? Warm up by adding the correct punctuation mark to each sentence in the paragraph below.

Do you hate getting shots   Many doctors give folks a shot to protect them against the flu virus   Now there is another choice   People can spray a vaccine called FluMist into their nose and avoid the needle   The government says FluMist is safe for healthy people ages 5 to 49   It costs about $50 a dose, and that price is about three to four times as much as a normal flu shot   Ouch

TFK Tips for Writers

Read aloud the paragraph above. How does your voice change when you read interrogative sentences? when you read exclamatory sentences?

Making Connections

You can show how ideas are related by combining two sentences to form a **compound sentence.** Use conjunctions, or connecting words, such as *and, but,* and *or.*

> Jim can go hiking with his family.　　He can play soccer with his friends.

> Jim can go hiking with his family, **or** he can play soccer with his friends.

A **run-on sentence** results when two or more sentences are put together without any punctuation. One way to correct a run-on is to make it a compound sentence. You can also add punctuation to form two separate sentences.

> **Run-on:** Tracey sent an email Carol replied with a telephone call.

> **Correction:** Tracey sent an email, **but** Carol replied with a telephone call.

> **Correction:** Tracey sent an email. Carol replied with a telephone call.

Try This!

Show how you would correct each of the run-on sentences below.

1 I like reading mysteries my sister prefers adventure stories.

_____

2 The wind was howling the shutters were banging against the windows.

_____

3 The class will visit the science museum the students will attend a play downtown.

_____

Writing a Paragraph

A **paragraph** is a group of related sentences about one important idea. Good writers use paragraphs to organize their ideas as they write.

Parts of a Paragraph

Each paragraph includes a **topic sentence** that introduces the subject and tells the main idea. **Detail sentences** usually follow the topic sentence. They support and develop the main idea. A paragraph ends with a **concluding sentence** that finishes the paragraph.

Neither wind nor snow nor even school can keep volunteers in Aniak, Alaska, from racing to the rescue of injured people who need their help. ← Topic sentence

The Dragon Slayers—seven girls and two boys, all between the ages of 13 and 18—are an emergency medical team. They are on call around the clock. The team, led by volunteer fire chief Pete Brown, is the only 24-hour rescue service for an area about the size of Maryland. They respond to about 400 calls a year and serve about 2,000 people who live outside of Anchorage. ← Supporting detail sentences

The crew has already provided invaluable assistance, rescuing victims of snowmobile accidents, people trapped in fires, and plane-crash survivors. ← Concluding sentence

Try This!

Read the paragraph below, and then write an appropriate topic sentence on the lines at the beginning of the paragraph. Make sure that your sentence tells the main idea.

_____

_____

First, carefully stroke the needle with the bar magnet, moving from the middle toward the point, about ten times. Then put the needle on the cork and place it on the surface of the bowl of water. Watch as the cork turns until the needle is pointing north! If you have a commercial compass, use it to test the accuracy of your new compass.

Time to Edit

Look back at a piece of recent writing, and ask yourself the following questions:
- Does each paragraph have a clear opening statement?
- Do all the ideas in the paragraph relate to the main topic?
- Does each paragraph have a strong closing statement?

If you answered "no," to any of the questions, go back and fix the problem.

Focus on Capital Letters

Good writers know that certain words begin with capital letters. Refer to the chart below to help you find and fix capitalization errors in your writing.

First word in a sentence	**My** soccer team practices every day.
Proper nouns, such as the **names of people, places, companies,** and **organizations**	**Greta** and **Ula** are visiting from **Norway.** Members of the **World Wildlife Federation** work to protect animals.
Pronoun /	Angela and **I** are friends.
Titles (with a name) and their abbreviations	**Governor Thompson** will run for reelection. I visit **Mrs. Warner** every afternoon.
Days of the week, months, and **holidays**	**Martin Luther King, Jr. Day** falls on the third **Monday** in **January.**
Proper adjectives	Dr. Martin studied **South American** culture.
First, last, and important words in a title	*Harry Potter* and the *Goblet* of *Fire* is a fantastic book.

Try This!

Read the sentences. Circle words that should begin with a capital letter.

1 The ford motor company built the first popular car in the united states.

2 many americans dress up for halloween in october.

3 The state of kentucky was the birthplace of abraham lincoln.

Time to Edit

Read a paragraph or story you have written. Check to be sure that you have used capital letters correctly.

Focus on Punctuation

Punctuation marks help readers make sense of written text.

Quotation Marks

Narrative writing often includes dialogue. Writers use quotation marks to show the speakers' exact words. A comma is used to separate the quotation from the rest of the sentence.

> Dad whispered, "Look at the rainbow."

> "It's beautiful," Sarah replied. "Maybe the storm has ended."

Try This!

Add punctuation to the following dialogue.

What are you doing this weekend asked Julie.

The county fair starts on Friday answered Amy. Maybe Dad will take us.

That's a great idea Julie exclaimed.

Apostrophes

Writers use apostrophes to show ownership. For singular nouns, add an apostrophe and s ('s).

the bike that belongs to **Aaron**	**Aaron's** bike
the tail that belongs to the **puppy**	the **puppy's** tail
the cover of the **book**	the **book's** cover

For plural nouns that end with s, just add an apostrophe (').

the skates that belong to the **girls**	the **girls'** skates
the color of the **tulips**	the **tulips'** color

73

Commas

Commas tell a reader to pause briefly before reading on. Look at how commas are used in the following examples.

Words in a series	You'll need paper, scissors, and markers for this project.
To separate adjectives	The plump, agile cat leapt from the chair.
Before the conjunction in a compound sentence	Lisa set the table, and Brian made some sandwiches.
Between a city and state, or a city and country	The Baseball Hall of Fame is in Cooperstown, New York. It is my dream to visit Paris, France.
To separate a noun in direct address	Anita, please read your story. You did a great job, Jack!

Try This!

Read the paragraph below. Place the correct punctuation marks where they belong.

My name is Maria E Harris I enjoy swimming playing basketball and doing crossword puzzles I traveled with my family to India when I was 8 years old We saw the Taj Mahal and it was magnificent That was an amazing trip Would you like to go to India some day

Time to Edit

Look at something you are writing. Check to be sure all sentences are correctly punctuated.

Check Your Spelling

When you spell words correctly, it is easier for others to read and understand what you write. Correct spelling allows readers to focus on your message. Many words have spelling patterns like those in the words listed below.

Form plurals				
book	dress	beach	fox	shelf
books	dresses	beaches	foxes	shelves

Add suffixes -ed and -ing			
kick	pour	flap	move
kicked	poured	flapped	moved
kicking	pouring	flapping	moving

Add -es, -ed, -er, -est to words ending with a consonant + y			
country	identify	healthy	easy
countries	identified	healthier	easiest

Add suffix -ion		
inspect	introduce	proceed
inspection	introduction	procession

Common ending sounds
postage
creative
practice
mountain
adventure

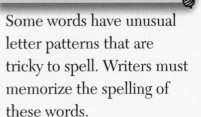

Final /l/ sound spelled le, el, al		
dazzle	flannel	mental

TFK Tips for Writers

Some words have unusual letter patterns that are tricky to spell. Writers must memorize the spelling of these words.

Try This!

Circle the spelling mistakes in the sentences below. Rewrite the sentences correctly on a separate sheet of paper.

1 The direcshuns say to meazur two cups of flour.

2 Dan wrote an amuseing story about wolfs.

3 Did you notis that the new printer is defectiv?

Time to Edit

Proofread something you have written. Circle words you are unsure of and check their spellings in the dictionary.

Using Proofreading Marks

Once you have revised your first draft, it's time to find and fix any mistakes. All writers and editors use a special set of marks to show what changes need to be made.

Common Proofreading Marks

≡	Make capital	⊙	Add a period	¶	Start a new paragraph
/	Make lowercase	⋏	Add a comma	ℓ	Delete a letter or word
∧	Insert a letter or a word	# ∧	Insert a space	⋎	Insert an apostrophe

Try This!

Look at the proofreading marks in the paragraph below. Why were these changes made?

¶ Last summer my family and I went to Sydney, australia. I had read a travel book called _The Kid's Book of Australia_, so I had a list of Places I wanted to visit. We visited a really cool natural history museum that had bones that were millions of years old. We took a long ferry ride⊙ We also went to a wildlife park where we saw koalas kangaroos and wombats. My sister and I hope we can got back to Australia for our next family vacation.

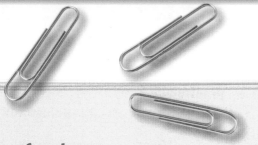

Tips for Proofreaders

Here are a few suggestions for finding and fixing mistakes in your writing.

Before you proofread, set your writing aside for a couple of hours. You will be more likely to catch mistakes if you take a break and return to your writing with a clear, fresh mind.

Read what you have written aloud. This is a great way to "hear" whether your writing makes sense.

Use a ruler or a piece of paper to help train your eyes on one line of writing at a time. If your eyes are focused only on one line, your brain is likely to stay focused, too.

Read what you have written from end to beginning instead of from beginning to end. This technique allows you to concentrate on the letters, words, and punctuation marks. You'll see what is actually on the page, not what you expect to be there.

TFK Tips for Writers

Do you need to proofread even if you write with a computer? Yes! Computer spell-check programs catch some mistakes, but not all of them.

Time to Edit

Proofread something you have written. Use the checklist to help you find your mistakes. Use proofreading marks to identify and correct the errors. Then make the necessary changes and write a final copy.

remember to proofread

Try This!

Proofread the passage carefully. Use proofreading marks to show the mistakes you find.

Proofreader's Checklist

Here is a checklist you can use whenever you proofread.

☐ I wrote complete sentences.

☐ I checked my writing for correct grammar.

☐ I indented all paragraphs.

☐ I used capital letters and lowercase letters correctly.

☐ I used italics or underlines for titles of books, movies, and television shows.

☐ I checked my writing for errors in punctuation.

☐ I checked my writing for misspelled words.

☐ I made a neat final copy of my writing.

How does elementary school teacher Kay tolliver get her students excited about math She uses all sorts of unusual tactics, like dressing in costumes or working with props, to teach her students too solve real-life problems with math Now millions of TV viewers can learn math while waching Tolliver's antics on The Eddie Files, a PBS program shehosts.

5

Publishing

Time to write your
final copy and share
it with others

What to Publish

Writers publish their work when they present their best pieces of writing for others to enjoy. When good writers practice their craft, they may produce several drafts before they have a piece that is ready to publish. But how do writers decide when to publish their work? Here are some questions you can ask yourself to help make that decision.

To Publish or Not to Publish

- Do I want to share this piece of writing with others? Why?

- Does my writing have a specific purpose? Does it inform, describe, explain, persuade, or simply entertain?

- Do I express my ideas clearly? Does this piece accomplish my purpose?

- Does my writing suit my audience? Will it hold readers' interest?

- Is there any part I want to change before I publish it? Does my piece seem like it is "finished"?

- After I read the piece, do I feel good about the job I've done?

TFK Tips for Writers

There are many different ways to publish, or share, your written work. For example, you might present your work by giving a speech, creating a visual display, or acting out your story.

Read on to explore more ideas for publishing.

Publishing Your Final Draft

Remember that when it comes to publishing, you have many choices beyond simply writing your words down on paper. Think about how you might present your writing, and try to come up with a creative solution. Look below for ideas on different ways to publish your writing and suggestions for when to use them. Can you think of any other imaginative ways to share your work with others?

- Fictional story
- Drama
- Historical narrative

Role-play the story.

- Informational report
- Persuasive essay
- Autobiography

Make an oral presentation.

- Opinion piece
- News article
- Letter to the editor

Publish in a print or online newspaper.

Ways to Publish

Create a video clip.

- News article
- Book review
- Editorial

Put together a class book or newsletter.

- Response to literature
- Fictional story
- Personal narrative

Design a poster to illustrate your writing.

- Informational report
- How-to piece
- Cause-and-effect essay

Publishing on a Computer

You may decide to publish your writing using a computer. Use these features to give your writing a neat, professional appearance.

Step 1: Format

Choose a type style and size that will make your words easy to read. You can emphasize certain ideas by using **bold** or *italic* type. Varying the font and size of the letters adds interest to the pages. Remember, though, that using too many different fonts can interfere with what you are trying to say.

Raccoon Report

Helvetica (10-point)

Helvetica (12-point)

Times Italic (12-point)

Times Bold (12-point)

Times Bold (14 point)

Step 2: Add Art

Art and accompanying captions help readers get a clearer picture of the information being presented. There are different ways to include visuals and images in your writing.

- Use the computer's Draw feature to create an original picture.
- Add clip art to illustrate ideas.

Step 3: Include Tables and Charts

Tables, charts, and graphs present specific information at a glance. Most word-processing programs provide a variety of tables that have already been formatted. Just fill in the data and create a title. You also can make bar graphs, line graphs, and pie charts.

Step 4: Print, Save, and File

After you have completed your document, save it, then print out a final copy. When you save it, give your work a descriptive file name. You might create a separate electronic folder to store each kind of writing, such as one for narrative fiction and one for poetry. This will help you review your writing and keep track of your progress.

Planning a Multimedia Presentation

Another publishing idea that some writers use combines several of the methods already described. You may choose to create a **multimedia presentation,** a way of publishing on the computer that combines words, pictures, and sounds. Creating this kind of presentation enables you to express your ideas more effectively than you can with words alone. Use the following guidelines to help you design a multimedia presentation.

Getting the Equipment

Before beginning preparation for a multimedia presentation, make sure you have all the necessary equipment:

- a personal computer with a large memory
- high-quality video and audio systems
- a CD-ROM drive
- a multimedia software program

Other equipment is helpful as well:

- a digital camera
- a video recorder
- a scanner
- high-speed Internet access

Creating the Presentation

A multimedia presentation can include several components, such as words, images, sound, and animation.

Words

Multimedia presentations include words, just as written reports and stories do. However, special features are available that can add interest and meaning to your words. Multimedia software will also help you arrange the text so it makes a powerful impact on the computer screen. Here are some techniques to try.

- Use bulleted lists to highlight key ideas.
- Show important words and phrases in bold or italic print.
- Add captions to photos and images.

Images and Videos

Including carefully chosen images in your presentation will help you tell a story or convey detailed information in a clear, understandable way. Pictures can also grab the attention of your audience and keep them interested in your topic. Here are some ideas for using images.

- Scan photographs or art.
- Generate your own art with computer programs.
- Use a video recorder to film scenes for your presentation.
- Download available clips from the Internet that include video you cannot capture yourself.

Sound

Adding sound to your presentation can create a mood and make your writing seem more realistic. Here are some ideas for using sound in your presentation.

- Download short sound clips from the Internet to suggest the setting of the presentation.
- Write a script and ask friends or family to read the text aloud.
- Add introductory music to the opening of your presentation.

Animation

Animation software allows you to create people and objects that are important to your topic and bring them to life on the computer. You can use animation to create a variety of special effects.

- Show how something moves or changes.
- Draw a plant and show how it blossoms.
- Present a narrative through animated characters.

Time to Publish

Choose something you have written and use it to create a multimedia presentation or other kind of presentation that showcases your writing. Share your presentation with your class or with others who would be interested in your topic.

Vocabulary

Time to think
about the words
you use

Words to Write With

There are close to 200,000 words that English speakers use in day-to-day life! With all these words to chose from, how do writers pick the best word? They try many different words until they find the perfect one to communicate a description, feeling, or mood. Use these lists to help you choose good words. Add your own favorites to the words in each list, too.

Frequently Used Words

1. activity
2. amaze
3. athlete
4. beverage
5. celebrate
6. difficult
7. environment
8. possession
9. situation
10. typical
11. unbelievable
12. valuable

Time to Write

Make a list of words you often use in your writing or would like to use more often.

1 _____

2 _____

3 _____

4 _____

Fantastic Adjectives

1. brilliant
2. enormous
3. fiery
4. frantic
5. miniature
6. outlandish
7. quaint
8. revolutionary
9. rugged
10. scarlet
11. shabby
12. sly

Time to Write

Make a list of unusual adjectives. Use them to make your descriptions come alive.

1 _____

2 _____

3 _____

4 _____

Vivid Verbs

1. crouch
2. glare
3. hurl
4. inhabit
5. jostle
6. lob
7. lurk
8 scamper
9. slither
10. snarl
11. tumble
12. wallow

Time to Write

Vivid verbs help create a picture in your reader's head. Make a list of some vivid verbs you like.

1 _____

2 _____

3 _____

4 _____

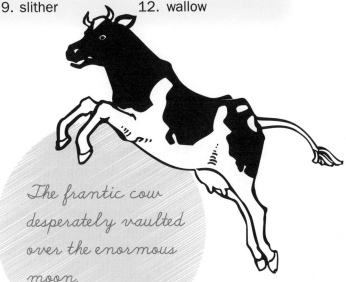

The frantic cow desperately vaulted over the enormous moon.

Lively Adverbs

1. abruptly
2. adoringly
3. desperately
4. gingerly
5. greedily
6. gustily
7. longingly
8. mischievously
9. miserably
10. reluctantly
11. tenderly
12. unexpectedly

Time to Write

Lively adverbs tell your reader more about an action. Write down four adverbs, and use them in your next story.

1 _____   3 _____

2 _____   4 _____

Rhyming Words

1. zoom	3. true	5. brown	7. spring	9. feet
gloom	blue	gown	king	sweet
broom	few	town	wing	bleat
2. light	4. throw	6. gray	8. wall	10. bought
bright	glow	today	fall	caught
tonight	pillow	away	recall	fought

Time to Write

These sets of rhyming words all belong to word families.
Make lists of word families that you can use for writing poetry.

1 _____   3 _____

2 _____   4 _____

Frequently Misspelled Words

1. beautiful	4. different	7. favorite	10. through
2. cinnamon	5. embarrassment	8. receive	11. until
3. college	6. exaggeration	9. separate	12. usually

Time to Write

Check the spelling of words you are unsure of. Then write them below.

1 _____   3 _____

2 _____   4 _____

More Words to Write With

As you explore different topics for your writing, you will need a variety of words at your fingertips. Look at the word lists on these pages. Can you think of a time when you might use these words?

Citizenship and Community

1. duty	4. justice	7. plaza	10. senator
2. election	5. metropolitan	8. resident	11. sheriff
3. jury	6. patriot	9. responsibility	12. suburb

Time to Write

Make a list of other words about your community. Include these words in stories and reports that describe life in the United States.

1 _____　3 _____

2 _____　4 _____

Family and Friends

1. acquaintance	4. companion	7. guardian	10. relative
2. ancestor	5. cousin	8. niece	11. reunion
3. buddy	6. grandparent	9. pal	12. sibling

Time to Write

Make a list of other words that will help you write stories and essays about the relationship among family members and friends.

1 _____　3 _____

2 _____　4 _____

Professions

1. archaeologist	4. gardener	7. musician	10. professor
2. astronomer	5. lawyer	8. physician	11. social worker
3. firefighter	6. mechanic	9. plumber	12. veterinarian

Time to Write

Make a list of other words that identify the work that people do. Use these lists to brainstorm ideas for characters' careers.

1 _____

2 _____

3 _____

4 _____

Feelings and Emotions

1. anxious	4. courageous	7. generous	10. ridiculous
2. astonished	5. enthusiastic	8. melancholy	11. sensitive
3. confident	6. jealous	9. persnickety	12. serene

Time to Write

Make a list of other words that name feelings and emotions. Use these words to describe characters in biographies and narratives.

1 _____   3 _____

2 _____   4 _____

Imagination and Adventure

1. backpack	4. emperor	7. fortress	10. stagecoach
2. detective	5. expedition	8. parachute	11. wilderness
3. emergency	6. fingerprint	9. shipwreck	12. wizard

Time to Write

Make a list of other words that describe real and imaginary experiences that people have. Include these words in adventure stories, mysteries, historical stories, and fantasies.

1 _____

2 _____

3 _____

4 _____

Transportation and Geography

1. ferry	4. prairie	7. spacecraft	10. thicket
2. mesa	5. rain forest	8. subway	11. underground
3. mountaintop	6. reef	9. swamp	12. vehicle

Time to Write

Make a list of other words about places and travel. Look at the lists to create realistic settings for your stories.

1 _____ 3 _____

2 _____ 4 _____

Index

A

Action words. *See* Verbs
Active voice, 62
Adjectives, 63
    fantastic, 86
    proper, 72
Adventure, 22, 27
    words for, 91
Adverbs, 64
    lively, 87
Almanac, 34
Animation, 84
Apostrophes, 73
Art
    for published writing, 82, 84
Atlas, 19
Audience, 9, 12, 20, 44, 46, 47,
    54, 80
Autobiography
    publishing, 81

B

Beginnings, 56–57. *See also*
    Openings
Bold type, 82
Book review
    publishing, 81

C

Capitalization, 7, 11, 72
Cause and Effect Diagram, 22
Cause-and-effect essay, 38
    publishing, 81
Characters, 28
    creating, 29, 30, 31
Checklists
    for interview, 43
    for nonfiction, 40
    for proofreading, 78

for spelling, 75
for a story, 31
for writing to persuade, 47
Cinquains, 52
Citizenship
    words for, 89
Closings
    strong and weak, 49
Command. *See* Imperative
    sentence
Commas, 74
Community
    words for, 89
Compound predicate, 66
Compound subject, 66
Computer
    using in publishing, 82–84
Concluding sentence, 70
Concrete poem, 51
Conventions
    capitalization, 7, 11, 72
    editing and proofreading, 7,
        11, 66–78
    publishing, 7, 12, 80–84
    punctuation, 7, 11, 73–74
    spelling, 7, 11, 30, 75, 88

D

Days of the week
    capitals for, 72
Declarative sentence, 67
    punctuation for, 67
Description
    as opening, 48, 56
Design
    of published writing, 82
Details, 29–30, 35, 39
Detail sentences, 70
Dialogue, 28, 30
    punctuating, 73

Dictionary, 34
Drafting, 6, 9, 24–52
    fiction, 26–31
    first draft, 9, 24–25, 54
    nonfiction, 32–49
    poetry, 50–52
Drama
    publishing, 81

E

ed endings, 75
Editing and proofreading, 7, 11,
    66–78
    checklist for, 75, 78
    marks for, 11, 76
    tips for proofreaders, 77
Editorial
    publishing, 81
Emotions
    words for, 90
Encyclopedia, 19, 34
Essay, 38–40
Exact nouns, 61
Examples, 40, 44, 45
Exclamatory sentence, 67–68
    punctuation for, 67
Exclamation point, 67
Experience Chart, 22

F

Facts, 36–37, 44–45
Family
    words for, 89
Fantastic adjectives, 86
Feelings
    words for, 90
Fiction, 26–31
    adventure story, 27
    character details, 29
    checklist for, 31

legends, 26
myths, 26
publishing, 81
science fiction, 27
story elements, 28–31
File command, 82
First draft, 9, 24–25, 54. *See also* Drafting
sample, 25
Fonts
for published writing, 82
Fragments. *See* Sentences, fragments
Frequently misspelled words, 88
Frequently used words, 86
Friends
words for, 89

G

Geography
words for, 91
Graphic Organizers, 8, 19, 21, 22, 45

H

Historical narrative
publishing, 81
Holidays
capitals for, 72
How-to-article, 33
publishing, 81

I

Idea map, 8
Ideas
details in, 35, 59
in drafting, 6, 9, 24
facts, 36
gathering, 16–17
information sources, 19, 34
opinions, 36–37
organizing, 45
in prewriting, 6, 8, 14–22
topics, 6, 8, 15–19

Images, 84
Imagination
words for, 91
Imperative sentence, 67
punctuation for, 67
Information
locating sources, 19, 34
Informational report
publishing, 81
ing endings, 75
Internet, 19, 34
Interrogative sentence, 67
punctuation for, 67
Interview, 41–43
checklist for, 43
-*ion* endings, 75
Italic type, 82

L

Legends, 26
Letter to the editor
publishing, 81
Limericks, 50
Lists
for ideas, 16–17
Lively adverbs, 87

M

Main idea, 21, 35
main idea organizer, 21
Making connections
editing and proofreading, 69
Mapping. *See* Idea map
Meaning
idea order and, 58
Months
capitals for, 72
Multimedia presentation, 83–84
Myths, 26

N

Names of people and places
capitals for, 72

Narrative
fiction, 26–27
nonfiction, 32
personal, 22, 32
News article
publishing, 81
Newspaper
publishing, 81
Nonfiction, 19, 32–49
checklists for, 40, 43, 47
essay, 38–40
information source, 19, 34
how-to-article, 33
interview, 41–43
narrative, 32
openings and closings, 48
personal narrative, 32
poetry, 50–52
writing to persuade, 44–47
Note-taking, 15
Nouns, 61
proper, 72

O

Openings. *See also* Beginnings
strong, 48
Opinion, 36
in persuasive essay, 8
publishing essay, review, or editorial, 80
Opinion piece
publishing, 81
Oral presentation
publishing, 81
Organization
in drafting, 39–40
editing, 69–71
main idea, 21
of persuasive writing, 45
in prewriting, 8, 21–22
revising for, 58–59
of sentences, 30
sequence, 21
word order, 60

P

Paragraphs, 70
    order of sentences, 70–71
    parts of, 70
    transitions, 39–40
Parts of a sentence, 66
Parts of a story, 28
Passive voice, 62
Patterns
    in poetry, 50, 52
    sound and letter, 50
Periods, 67
Personal narrative, 22, 32
    publishing, 81
Persuasive essay, 8, 44–47
    checklist for, 47
    publishing, 81
Planning
    in prewriting, 20
Plot, 28, 30
Plurals, 75
Poetry, 50–52
Point of view
    in persuasive essay, 8
Predicate. *See* Sentences,
    predicates
Presentation
    appearance and, 82
    on a computer, 82, 83–84
    publishing for, 84
    visuals for, 84
Prewriting, 6, 8, 14–22
    choosing a topic, 18
    ideas in, 6, 8, 14–17
    narrowing a topic, 19
    organizing ideas, 8, 21–22
    think and plan, 6, 20
    web, 8
Print command, 82
Professions
    words for, 90
Pronouns
    capitalization, 72
Proofreading. *See* Editing and
    proofreading

Proper adjectives, 72
    Proper nouns. *See* Nouns,
        proper
Publishing, 7, 12, 80–84
    appearance and, 82
    on a computer, 82
    of final draft, 81
    multimedia presentation, 83
    print, save, and file, 82
    visuals for, 82–84
    ways to publish, 81
Punctuation, 7, 67, 73–74

Q

Question marks, 67
Questions
    for ideas, 20
    as opening, 48, 56
    sentence as, 67
Quotation
    as opening, 56
Quotation marks, 73

R

Readers' responses, 9, 12, 20, 54
Reference works. *See*
    Information, locating sources
Report, 81
    publishing, 81
Responses to literature
    publishing, 81
Revising, 7, 10, 54–78
    adjectives, 63
    adverbs, 64
    beginnings, 56–57
    for meaning, 58–59
    nouns, 61
    verbs, 62
    word order, 60
Rhyme
    in poetry, 50
Rhyming words, 88
Rhythm
    in poetry, 50
Run-on sentences, 69

S

Save command, 82
Science fiction, 27
Sentence fluency
    drafting, 6, 9, 23–52
    editing and proofreading, 7,
        11, 65–78
    revising, 7, 10, 53–64
Sentences, 66–69. *See also*
    Fluency
    capitalization in, 72
    closing, 49
    combining, 54, 69
    compound, 69
    fragments, 66
    opening, 48
    organizing, 30
    parts of, 66
    predicates, 66
    punctuating, 67–68, 73–74
    run-on, 69
    stringy, 67–68
    subjects, 66
    types of, 67–68, 70
    word order in, 60
Sequence organizer, 21
Setting, 28, 30
Six Traits Plus One. *See*
    Conventions; Fluency;
    Ideas; Organization;
    Publishing; Voice; Word
    Choice
Sound, 84
Sound patterns
    word endings, 75
Sound words
    in poetry, 50, 52
Spelling, 7, 11, 30
    frequently misspelled words,
        88
Statement
    punctuation for, 67
    sentence as, 67

Story
    checklist for, 31
    elements of, 28–31
    parts of, 28
    publishing, 81
Stringy sentence, 67
Subject. *See* Sentences, subjects
Suffixes, 75
Supporting details, 35, 59
Syllables, 75
Symbols
    proofreading, 11, 76

T

Tables and charts
    for published writing, 82
Technology
    words for, 25
Theme. *See* Topic
Thesaurus, 34, 62
Time order words, 58
Time to Edit, 66, 68, 71, 72, 74,
    75, 78
Time to Publish, 84
Time to Revise, 54, 57, 59, 61,
    62, 63, 64
Time to Write, 17, 28, 29, 31,
    33, 37, 40, 43, 44 , 47, 49,
    50, 51, 55, 56, 86, 87, 88,
    89, 90, 91
Tips for Writers, 15, 18, 19, 21,
    55, 62, 67, 68, 69, 70, 75
    for Fiction Writers, 27, 28
    for Nonfiction Writers, 32,
        33, 34, 37, 40, 42, 46, 47
    for Poetry Writers, 52
    from a Pro, 9, 10, 24, 35, 43,
        54, 56
    for Proofreaders, 77
    for Publishing, 80
    Using Writer's Voice, 8
    Writing Process, 7
Titles, 18, 55
    capitals for, 72
    of people, 72

Topic
    choosing, 18
    narrowing, 19
    think and plan about, 20
Topic sentence, 35, 70
Topic Web, 8
Traits of Good Writing. *See*
        Conventions; Fluency;
        Ideas; Organization;
        Publishing; Voice; Word
        Choice
Transitions, 39–40, 58
Transportation
    words for, 91
Triangle organizer, 45
Type sizes
    for published writing, 82

U

Unexpected statement
    as opening, 48

V

Verbs, 62
    vivid, 62, 87
Verse, 50
Videos, 84
Viewpoint organizer, 45
Visuals, 84
    in multimedia
        presentation, 84
    as opening, 48
    for published writing, 82
Vivid verbs, 62, 87
Vocabulary, 86–91
Voice
    active, 62
    drafting for, 6, 9, 31, 32, 40,
        41, 46, 47, 48, 49
    passive, 62
    prewriting for, 6, 8, 20
    revising for, 54, 61–64

W

Web sites. *See* Internet
Word choice
    adjectives, 63, 86
    adverbs, 64, 88
    citizenship, 89
    community, 89
    drafting and, 31, 33, 43
    family, 89
    feelings and emotions, 90
    frequently misspelled
        words, 88
    frequently used words, 86
    friends, 89
    imagination and
        adventure, 91
    for multimedia
        presentation, 83
    professions, 89
    revising and, 60, 61–64
    space and technology, 25
    strong nouns, 61
    time order, 58
    transportation and
        geography, 91
    vivid verbs, 62
    vocabulary and, 85–91
Word endings, 75
Word order, 60
Word poems, 51
Writer's notebook, 5, 14
Writing process, 6–12
    drafting, 6, 9, 24–52
    editing and proofreading, 7,
        11, 66–78
    prewriting, 6, 8, 14–22
    publishing, 7, 12, 80–84
    revising, 7, 10, 54–64
Writing to persuade, 44–47
    checklist for, 47

Traits of Good Writing Index

Ideas
details, 35, 59
in drafting, 6, 9, 24
facts, 36
gathering, 16–17
information sources, 19, 34
opinions, 36
organizing, 45
in prewriting, 6, 8, 14–22
topics, 6, 8, 15–19

Organization
in drafting, 6, 9, 28, 32, 33,
    38, 39–40
editing, 69–71
main idea, 21
of persuasive writing, 45
in prewriting, 8, 21–22
revising for, 58–59
of sentences, 30
sequence, 21
word order, 60

Voice
active, 62
drafting for, 6, 9, 31, 32, 40,
    44, 46, 47, 48, 49
passive, 62
prewriting for, 6, 8, 20
revising for, 54, 61–64

Word choice
adjectives, 63, 86
adverbs, 64, 88
citizenship, 89
community, 89
drafting and, 31, 33, 43
family, 89
feelings and emotions, 90
frequently misspelled
    words, 88

frequently used words, 86
friends, 89
imagination and adventure,
    91
for multimedia presentation,
    83
professions, 89
revising and, 60, 61–64
space and technology, 25
strong nouns, 61
time order, 58
transportation and
    geography, 91
vivid verbs, 62
vocabulary and, 86–91

Sentence fluency
drafting, 6, 9, 24–52
editing and proofreading, 7,
    11, 66–78
revising, 7, 10, 54–64

Conventions
capitalization, 7, 11, 72
editing and proofreading, 7,
    11, 66–78
publishing, 7, 12, 80–84
punctuation, 7, 67, 73–74
spelling, 7, 11, 30, 88

Publishing, 7, 12, 80–84
appearance and, 82
on a computer, 82–84
of final draft, 81–84
multimedia presentation,
    83–84
print, save, and file, 82
visuals for, 82–84
ways to publish, 81